Travel Journal

Israel

VPJournals

Contact Details

Name: _____

Email address: _____

Tel: _____

Address: _____

_____

_____

Important Medical Information

Blood type: _____

Medication: _____

CONTENTS

Hi, I hope you enjoy this journal. It is packed with cool stuff and recommendations for you trip to Israel, and has plenty of space to record details of your trip.

Have fun in Israel

Great Places to visit in Israel

Dead Sea	✓
Church of the Holy Sepulchre	
Israel Museum	
Agamon HaHula	
Beit She'an National Park	
Baha'i Gardens and Golden Dome	
Mount of the Beatitudes	
Ancient Galilee Boat	
Beit Alpha Synagogue	
Western Wall	
Capernaum	
Dome of the Rock (al-Haram al-Sharif)	

Masada	
Hezekiah's Tunnel	
Gamla	
Beit She'arim	
Tabgha	
Tel Dan Nature Reserve	
Basilica of the Annunciation	
Belvoir	
Yehudiya Nature Reserve	
Sea of Galilee	
Bet Guvrin-Maresha National Park	
Hamat Gader Park	
Hecht Museum	

Cool Places to visit in Israel with Kids

Tel Aviv Museum of Art	✓
Masada Museum	
Hecht Museum	
Hula Nature Reserve	
Museum on the Seam	
Golan Archaeological Museum	
Ein Bokek Beach	
Knights Halls	
Coral Beach Nature Reserve	
En Avdat National Park	
Ice Space	
Shabbat of a Lifetime	

Old City of Jerusalem	
Mount of Olives	
Dolphin Reef	
Tower of David Museum	
Garden of Gethsemane	
Underwater Observatory Marine Park	
Palmach Museum	
Safari Park	
Israeli Children's Museum	
Yitzhak Rabin Center	
Tisch Family Zoological Gardens (Biblical Zoo)	
Museum of the Jewish People (Bet Hatefutsoth)	

Good Places to Eat in Israel

Ma'ayan HaBira	✓
HaMis'ada shel ImaKaparuc'hka	
Uri Buri	
Misedet HaArazim	
AlReda	
Yisrael's Kitchen	
Ktzeh HaNahal	
Dag Al HaDan	
Golan Brewhouse	
Faces	
Pastory	
Abu Ashraf	

HaBayit	
Shiri Bistro & Wine Bar	
Paulina IceCreamy	
Nalchik	
Darna	
Sudfeh	
Shirat Ro'im	
Hamarakia	
Chez Eugéne	
Little Jerusalem	
Amigo Emil	
Moshbutz	
Ein Camonim	

Best Websites to Research Further

Do some more research on the internet to plan your trip:

www.goisrael.com
www.govisitisrael.com
goisrael.about.com
www.thinkisrael.com
www.wikitravel.org/en/Israel
www.lonelyplanet.com/israel
www.touristisrael.com
www.wikipedia.org/wiki/Israel
www.israel-tourist-information.com
www.inisrael.com

More places I want to visit on our trip

1. _____

2. _____

3. _____

4. _____

5. _____

6. _____

7. _____

8. _____

9. _____

10. _____

11. _____

12. _____

13. _____

14. _____

15. _____

Postcard List

Name:
Address:

Name:
Address:

Name:
Address:

Name:

Address:

Name:

Address:

Name:

Address:

Name:

Address:

Name:

Address:

Name:

Address:

Name:

Address:

Name:

Address:

Name:

Address:

Name:

Address:

Name:

Address:

Packing List

✔	This Journal
	Tickets
	Passport
	Money
	Chargers
	Batteries
	Book to read
	Camera
	Tablet
	Sun glasses
	Sun cream

	Toiletries
	Water
	Watch
	Snacks
	Umbrella
	Towel
	Guide book
	Kindle
	Jacket
	Medication
	Add more below

Israel Facts

- Israel's two official languages are Hebrew and Arabic. Israel's financial center is Tel Aviv

- Jerusalem is the country's most populous city and its designated capital, although Israeli sovereignty over Jerusalem is not recognized internationally

- Israel is the world's only Jewish majority state; 6,110,600 citizens, or 75.3% of Israelis, are designated as Jewish

- The country's second largest groups of citizen are Arabs

- Israel has 137 official beaches (but only 273 km of coastline)

- The city of Beersheba has the highest number of chess grandmasters per capita in the world

- The Carmelit is one of the smallest subway systems in the world, having only four cars, six stations and a single tunnel 1.8 km (1.1 mi) long. The Carmelit is the only subway in Israel

- The Sea of Galilee located .212 km below sea level, is the lowest freshwater lake in the world and the largest in Israel

- The Dead Sea, also called the Salt Sea, is the lowest and the saltiest place on Earth's surface. People can easily float in the Dead Sea due to its unusually high salt concentration. It's almost impossible to dive into it

- The world's largest pepper was grown in Israel's Moshav Ein Yahav, as recorded by The Guinness Book of World Records in 2013

- Israel's national bird is the hoopoe. Eilat and the Hula Valley Reserve are some of the best bird-watching sites in the world. Israel's national flower is the Cyclamen persicum

- Israel shares land borders with Lebanon to the north, Syria in the northeast, Jordan on the east, the Palestinian territories comprising the West Bank and Gaza Strip on the east and southwest, respectively, and Egypt and the Gulf of Aqaba in the Red Sea to the south

- The earliest known archaeological artifact to mention the word "Israel" is the Merneptah Stele of ancient Egypt (dated to the late 13th century BCE)

- Motorola developed the cellphone and voice mail in Israel

- Jerusalem's Mount of Olives is the world's oldest continuously used cemetery

Clothes & Shoe Sizes

Children's Shoe Sizes

UK	EUROPE	US	Japan
4	20	4½ or 5	12 ½
4 ½	21	5 or 5½	13
5	21 or 22	5½ or 6	13 ½
5 ½	22	6	13½ or 14
6	23	6½ or 7	14 or 14½
6 ½	23 or 24	7 ½	14½ or 15
7	24	7½ or 8	15
7 ½	25	8 or 9	15 ½
8	25 or 26	8½ or 9	16
8 ½	26	9½	16 ½
9	27	9½ or 10	16 ½ or 17
10	28	10½ or 11	17 ½
10½ or 11	29	11½ or 12	18
11 ½	30	12½	18 or 18 ½
12	31	13	19 or 19 ½
12 ½	31	13 or 13½	19 ½ or 20
13	32	1	20
13 ½	32 ½	1 ½	20 ½
1	33	1½ or 2	21
2	34	2½ or 3	22

Children's Clothing Sizes

UK	EUROPE	US	Australia
12m	80cm	12-18m	12m
18m	80-86cm	18-24m	18m
24m	86-92cm	23-24m	2
2-3	92-98cm	2T	3
3-4	98-104cm	4T	4
3-5	104-110cm	5	5
5-6	110-116cm	6	6
6-7	116-122cm	6X-7	7
7-8	122-128cm	7 to 8	8
8-9	128-134cm	9 to 10	9
9-10	134-140cm	10	10
10-11	140-146cm	11	11
11-12	146-152cm	14	12

Women's Shoe Sizes

UK	EUROPE	US	Japan
3	35 ½	5	22 ½
3 ½	36	5 ½	23
4	37	6	23
4 ½	37 ½	6 ½	23 ½
5	38	7	24
5 ½	39	7 ½	24
6	39 ½	8	24 ½
6 ½	40	8 ½	25
7	41	9 ½	25 ½
7 ½	41 ½	10	26
8	42	10 ½	26 ½

Women's Clothes Sizes

UK	US	Japan	France / Spain	Germany	Israel	Australia
6/8	6	7-9	36	34	40	8
10	8	9-11	38	36	42	10
12	10	11-13	40	38	44	12
14	12	13-15	42	39	46	14
16	14	15-17	44	40	48	16
18	16	17-19	46	42	50	18
20	18	19-21	48	44	52	20

Men's Shoe Sizes

UK	EUROPE	US	Japan
6	38 ½	6 ½	24 ½
6 ½	39	7	25
7	40	7 ½	25 ½
7 ½	41	8	26
8	42	8 ½	27 ½
8 ½	43	9	27 ½
9	43 ½	9 ½	28
9 ½	44	10	28 ½
10	44	10 ½	28 ½
10 ½	44 ½	11	29
11	45	12	29 ½

Men's Suit / Coat / Sweater Sizes

UK / US / Aus	EU / Japan	General
32	42	Small
34	44	Small
36	46	Small
38	48	Medium
40	50	Large
42	52	Large
44	54	Extra Large
46	56	Extra Large

Men's Pants / Trouser Sizes (Waist)

UK / US	Europe
32	81 cm
34	86 cm
36	91 cm
38	97 cm
40	102 cm
42	107 cm

We have included another copy of this at the back of the book, so you can find it quickly again when you are in Israel

Israel Trip Diary

Write a daily diary during your trip

Day 1

Date: _____   **Weather:** _____

_____

_____

_____

_____

_____

_____

_____

_____

_____

_____

_____

_____

_____

Day 2

Date: _____   **Weather:** _____

Day 3

Date: _____   **Weather:** _____

Day 4

Date: _____   **Weather:** _____

Day 5

Date: _____   **Weather:** _____

_____

_____

_____

_____

_____

_____

_____

_____

_____

_____

_____

_____

_____

_____

Day 6

Date: _____   **Weather:** _____

Day 7

Date: _____   **Weather:** _____

Day 8

Date: _____   **Weather:** _____

Day 9

Date: _____   **Weather:** _____

Day 10

Date: _____   **Weather:** _____

Day 11

Date: _____   **Weather:** _____

Day 12

Date: _____   **Weather:** _____

Day 13

Date: _____   **Weather:** _____

Day 14

Date: _____   **Weather:** _____

Day 15

Date: _____   **Weather:** _____

Day 16

Date: ....   **Weather:** ....

Day 17

Date: _____ **Weather:** _____

Day 18

Date: _____   Weather: _____

_____

_____

_____

_____

_____

_____

_____

_____

_____

_____

_____

_____

_____

_____

Day 19

Date: _____   **Weather:** _____

Day 20

Date: _____   **Weather:** _____

Day 21

Date: **Weather:**

Memories of your Trip

Things I will remember from the trip

Favorite Places visited on the Trip

People I Met

Name:	
Address:	
Tel:	
email:	

Name:	
Address:	
Tel:	
email:	

Name:	
Address:	
Tel:	
email:	

Name:
Address:
Tel:
email:

Name:
Address:
Tel:
email:

Name:
Address:
Tel:
email:

Name:
Address:
Tel:
email:

Name:
Address:
Tel:
email:

Name:
Address:
Tel:
email:

Name:
Address:
Tel:
email:

Name:
Address:
Tel:
email:

We hope you enjoyed your trip to Israel

Please leave us a review if you found this Journal useful

Check out our useful resources on the next few pages

Clothes & Shoe Sizes

Children's Shoe Sizes

UK	EUROPE	US	Japan
4	20	4½ or 5	12 ½
4 ½	21	5 or 5½	13
5	21 or 22	5½ or 6	13 ½
5 ½	22	6	13½ or 14
6	23	6½ or 7	14 or 14½
6 ½	23 or 24	7 ½	14½ or 15
7	24	7½ or 8	15
7 ½	25	8 or 9	15 ½
8	25 or 26	8½ or 9	16
8 ½	26	9½	16 ½
9	27	9½ or 10	16 ½ or 17
10	28	10½ or 11	17 ½
10½ or 11	29	11½ or 12	18
11 ½	30	12½	18 or 18 ½
12	31	13	19 or 19 ½
12 ½	31	13 or 13½	19 ½ or 20
13	32	1	20
13 ½	32 ½	1 ½	20 ½
1	33	1½ or 2	21
2	34	2½ or 3	22

Children's Clothing Sizes

UK	EUROPE	US	Australia
12m	80cm	12-18m	12m
18m	80-86cm	18-24m	18m
24m	86-92cm	23-24m	2
2-3	92-98cm	2T	3
3-4	98-104cm	4T	4
3-5	104-110cm	5	5
5-6	110-116cm	6	6
6-7	116-122cm	6X-7	7
7-8	122-128cm	7 to 8	8
8-9	128-134cm	9 to 10	9
9-10	134-140cm	10	10
10-11	140-146cm	11	11
11-12	146-152cm	14	12

Women's Shoe Sizes

UK	EUROPE	US	Japan
3	35 ½	5	22 ½
3 ½	36	5 ½	23
4	37	6	23
4 ½	37 ½	6 ½	23 ½
5	38	7	24
5 ½	39	7 ½	24
6	39 ½	8	24 ½
6 ½	40	8 ½	25
7	41	9 ½	25 ½
7 ½	41 ½	10	26
8	42	10 ½	26 ½

Women's Clothes Sizes

UK	US	Japan	France / Spain	Germany	Israel	Australia
6/8	6	7-9	36	34	40	8
10	8	9-11	38	36	42	10
12	10	11-13	40	38	44	12
14	12	13-15	42	39	46	14
16	14	15-17	44	40	48	16
18	16	17-19	46	42	50	18
20	18	19-21	48	44	52	20

Men's Shoe Sizes

UK	EUROPE	US	Japan
6	38 ½	6 ½	24 ½
6 ½	39	7	25
7	40	7 ½	25 ½
7 ½	41	8	26
8	42	8 ½	27 ½
8 ½	43	9	27 ½
9	43 ½	9 ½	28
9 ½	44	10	28 ½
10	44	10 ½	28 ½
10 ½	44 ½	11	29
11	45	12	29 ½

Men's Suit / Coat / Sweater Sizes

UK / US / Aus	EU / Japan	General
32	42	Small
34	44	Small
36	46	Small
38	48	Medium
40	50	Large
42	52	Large
44	54	Extra Large
46	56	Extra Large

Men's Pants / Trouser Sizes (Waist)

UK / US	Europe
32	81 cm
34	86 cm
36	91 cm
38	97 cm
40	102 cm
42	107 cm

Common Translations

English	French	Spanish	Italian
Hello	Bonjour	Hola	Ciao
Goodbye	Au revoir	Adiós	Arrivederci
Yes	Oui	Sí	Si
No	Non	No	No
Please	S'il-vous-plaît	Por favor	Per favore
Thank you	Merci	Gracias	Grazie
Excuse me	Excusez-moi	Perdón	Mi scusi
How much	Combien	Cuánto	Quanto
My name is	Mon nom est	Mi nombre es	Io mi chiamo
Where is	Où est	Dónde está	Dov'è
The bank	La banque	El banco	La banca
The toilet	Les toilettes	El baño	Il bagno

German	Japanese	Mandarin	Hindi
Hallo	Kon'nichiwa	Ni hao	Namaste
Auf Wiedersehen	Sayonara	Zaijian	Alavida
Ja	Hai	Shi de	Ham
Nein	Ie	Meiyou	Nahim
Bitte	Onegaishimasu	Qing	Krpaya
Vielen Dank	Arigato	Xiexie	Dhan'yavada
Entschuldigung	Sumimasen	Duoshao	Mujhe mapha karem
Wie viel	Ikura	Wo de mingzi shi	Kitana
Mein Name ist	Watashinonamaeha	Nali	Mera nama hai
Wo ist	Doko ni aru	Yinhang	Kaham hai
Die Bank	Ginko	Yinhang	Bainka
Die Toilette	Toire	Cesuo	Saucalaya

Notes:

Made in the USA
San Bernardino, CA
16 December 2019